The MAILBOX®

For Every Learner 3

Reading & Vocabulary

3 Differentiated Activities for Every Skill

- Antonyms
- Cause and effect
- Context clues
- Drawing conclusions
- Fact and opinion
- Main idea and details

- Possessive nouns
- Prefixes
- Reading for details
- Suffixes
- Summarizing
- Synonyms

...And MORE!

Managing Editor: Jennifer Bragg

Editorial Team: Becky S. Andrews, Debbie Ashworth, Diane Badden, Kimberley Bruck, Karen A. Brudnak, Chris Curry, Lynette Dickerson, Tazmen Hansen, Marsha Heim, Lori Z. Henry, Angela Kamstra-Jacobson, Njeri Legrand, Debra Liverman, Kitty Lowrance, Dorothy C. McKinney, Thad H. McLaurin, Sharon Murphy, Jennifer Nunn, Mark Rainey, Hope Rodgers, Eliseo De Jesus Santos II, Rebecca Saunders, Barry Slate, Rachael Traylor, Zane Williard

Skill-building practice for today's learners!

www.themailbox.com

©2009 The Mailbox® Books
All rights reserved.
ISBN10 #1-56234-865-5 • ISBN13 #978-1-56234-865-6

Printed in the United States
10 9 8 7 6 5 4 3 2 1

Table of Contents

Practice each skill 3 different ways!

What's Inside

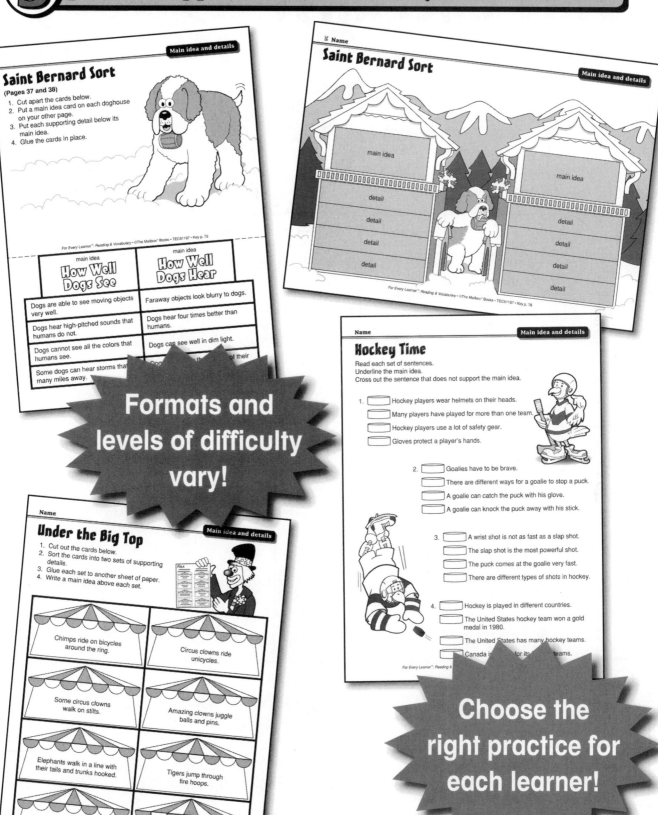

Saint Bernard Sort

(Pages 37 and 38)

1. Cut apart the cards below.
2. Put a main idea card on each doghouse on your other page.
3. Put each supporting detail below its main idea.
4. Glue the cards in place.

For Every Learner™: Reading & Vocabulary • ©The Mailbox® Books • TEC61187 • Key p. 78

main idea **How Well Dogs See**	main idea **How Well Dogs Hear**
Dogs are able to see moving objects very well.	Faraway objects look blurry to dogs.
Dogs hear high-pitched sounds that humans do not.	Dogs hear four times better than humans.
Dogs cannot see all the colors that humans see.	Dogs can see well in dim light.
Some dogs can hear storms that many miles away.	Dogs

Saint Bernard Sort — Main idea and details

Name

main idea

detail

detail

detail

detail

main idea

detail

detail

detail

detail

For Every Learner™: Reading & Vocabulary • ©The Mailbox® Books • TEC61187 • Key p. 78

Formats and levels of difficulty vary!

Hockey Time — Main idea and details

Name

Read each set of sentences.
Underline the main idea.
Cross out the sentence that does not support the main idea.

1. ☐ Hockey players wear helmets on their heads.
   ☐ Many players have played for more than one team.
   ☐ Hockey players use a lot of safety gear.
   ☐ Gloves protect a player's hands.

2. ☐ Goalies have to be brave.
   ☐ There are different ways for a goalie to stop a puck.
   ☐ A goalie can catch the puck with his glove.
   ☐ A goalie can knock the puck away with his stick.

3. ☐ A wrist shot is not as fast as a slap shot.
   ☐ The slap shot is the most powerful shot.
   ☐ The puck comes at the goalie very fast.
   ☐ There are different types of shots in hockey.

4. ☐ Hockey is played in different countries.
   ☐ The United States hockey team won a gold medal in 1980.
   ☐ The United States has many hockey teams.
   ☐ Canada is for its teams.

For Every Learner™: Reading &

Choose the right practice for each learner!

Under the Big Top — Main idea and details

Name

1. Cut out the cards below.
2. Sort the cards into two sets of supporting details.
3. Glue each set to another sheet of paper.
4. Write a main idea above each set.

Chimps ride on bicycles around the ring.	Circus clowns ride unicycles.
Some circus clowns walk on stilts.	Amazing clowns juggle balls and pins.
Elephants walk in a line with their tails and trunks hooked.	Tigers jump through fire hoops.
Sometimes dogs jump rope at the circus.	Circus clowns all squeeze into a small car.

40

For Every Learner™: Reading & Vocabulary • ©The Mailbox® Books • TEC61187 • Key p. 78

Skills Checklist

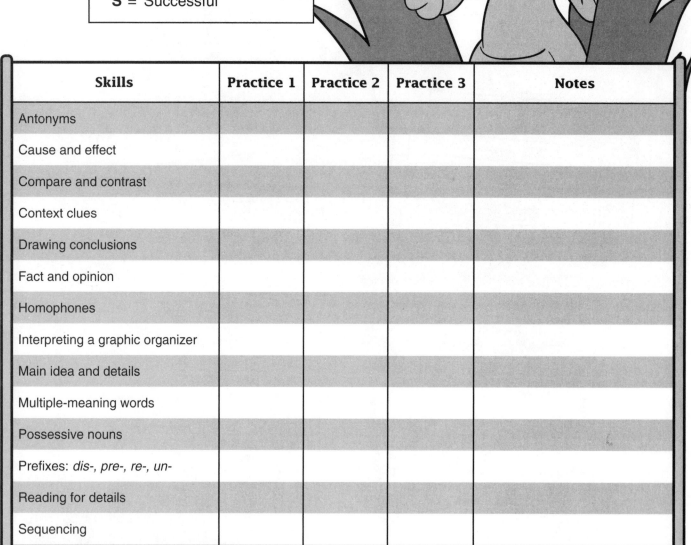

Assessment Code
M = More practice needed
S = Successful

Skills	Practice 1	Practice 2	Practice 3	Notes
Antonyms				
Cause and effect				
Compare and contrast				
Context clues				
Drawing conclusions				
Fact and opinion				
Homophones				
Interpreting a graphic organizer				
Main idea and details				
Multiple-meaning words				
Possessive nouns				
Prefixes: *dis-, pre-, re-, un-*				
Reading for details				
Sequencing				
Suffixes: *-able, -ly*				
Summarizing				
Synonyms				
Using a table of contents				

For Every Learner™: Reading & Vocabulary • ©The Mailbox® Books • TEC61187

Note to the teacher: To track the skill progress of individual students, personalize copies of the page. Each time a student completes a practice page, use the provided code to note an assessment of his work.

You're in Luck!

Cut apart the puzzle pieces below.
Match the word on each card with its antonym on the grid.
Glue.

above	add	best
come	friend	lucky
never	odd	same

For Every Learner™: Reading & Vocabulary • ©The Mailbox® Books • TEC61187 • Key p. 77

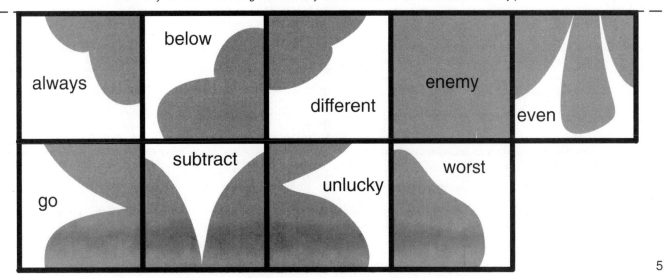

always	below	different	enemy	even
go	subtract	unlucky	worst	

In Training

(Pages 6 and 7)
Directions for two players:

1. Cut apart the cards below and the gameboards on your other page.
2. Stack the cards facedown and take a gameboard. Set the key aside.
3. When it's your turn, take a card and read the word aloud.
4. If you or your partner has the word's antonym on your gameboard, cover the space with a game marker. Then set the card aside.
5. The first player to cover four words in a row is the winner.

For Every Learner™: Reading & Vocabulary • ©The Mailbox® Books • TEC61187 • Key p. 77

1. north	2. awake	3. neat	4. huge
5. loose	6. true	7. bought	8. cheap
9. push	10. east	11. polite	12. dry
13. past	14. male	15. work	16. spend
17. multiply	18. private	19. heavy	20. attack
21. weak	22. possible	23. rough	24. brave

Note to the teacher: Refer to the answer key on page 77 to make an answer key for students to use as they play the game.

In Training

powerful	south	smooth	divide
asleep	afraid	present	false
sold	female	pull	untidy
public	play	guard	rude

In Training

afraid	tiny	west	tight
light	impossible	moist	play
earn	powerful	female	guard
smooth	divide	pull	expensive

For Every Learner™: Reading & Vocabulary • ©The Mailbox® Books • TEC61187 • Key p. 77

Different Ducks

1. Cut apart the cards below.
2. Match each pair of antonyms.
3. Glue the cards on another sheet of paper.

For Every Learner™: Reading & Vocabulary • ©The Mailbox® Books • TEC61187 • Key p. 77

accept	backward	careful	harmful
disagree	refuse	distant	exit
separate	borrow	fiction	forward
few	coward	hero	nonfiction
enter	join	lend	careless
many	agree	close	harmless

Time to Celebrate!

(Pages 9 and 10)

1. Cut apart the sentence strips below.
2. Place each cause strip next to its matching effect strip.
3. Glue the strips onto the cake on your other page.

For Every Learner™: Reading & Vocabulary • ©The Mailbox® Books • TEC61187 • Key p. 77

1. Jake can't sleep.	Sunday is Jake's birthday.
4. She will put nine candles on the cake.	Jake loves chocolate cake.
3. Jake's mom will bake a chocolate cake.	Jake will be nine years old.
2. There will be a party on Sunday.	He wants his wish to come true.
5. Jake will blow out all the candles.	He is excited about Sunday.

Name

Time to Celebrate!

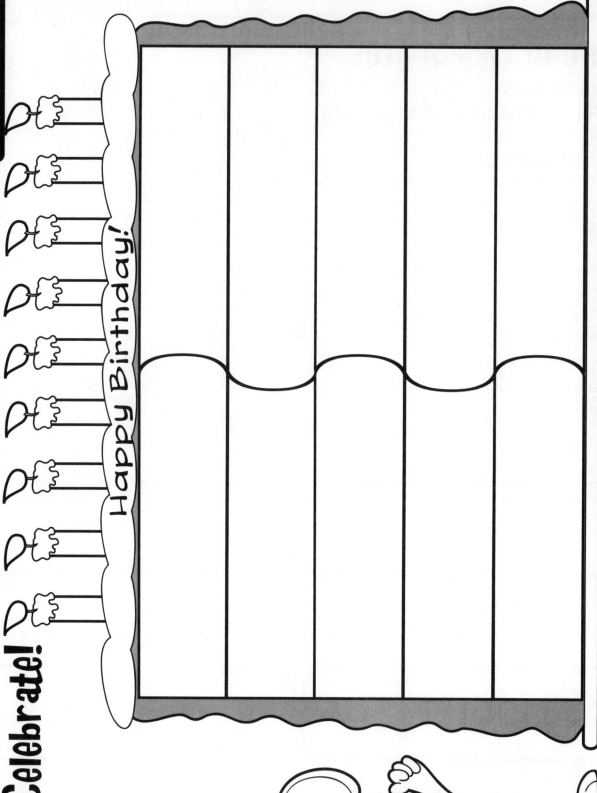

Happy Birthday!

For Every Learner™: Reading & Vocabulary • ©The Mailbox® Books • TEC61187 • Key p. 77

Note to the teacher: Use with "Time to Celebrate!" on page 9.

Happens for a Reason

Directions for two players:

1. Cut apart the cards below and stack them facedown.
2. When it's your turn, take the top card from the stack.
3. Read aloud both sentences. Have your partner tell which is the cause and which is the effect.
4. Check your partner's answers. If correct, he or she takes the card. If incorrect, return the card to the bottom of the stack.
5. After all cards have been played, the player with more cards wins.

For Every Learner™: Reading & Vocabulary • ©The Mailbox® Books • TEC61187

It's her birthday. **C** Beth is happy. **E**	The baby is crying. **E** The baby wants a bottle. **C**	He tripped. **E** Joe's shoelace was untied. **C**
Dad works very hard. **C** Dad gets a raise. **E**	Tim forgot his homework. **E** Tim didn't pack his backpack. **C**	I told my friend a joke. **C** My friend laughed. **E**
Dan went to bed early. **E** Dan felt tired. **C**	The floor is dirty. **C** Mom mops the floor. **E**	Our team celebrated. **E** Our team won the ball game. **C**
Ben studied every night. **C** Ben passed the test. **E**	The boy practices every day. **C** The boy plays the piano well. **E**	The teacher helps the student. **E** The student can't find the answer. **C**
Meg's feet are cold. **C** Meg puts on warm socks. **E**	Jan has paint on her hands. **C** Jan washes her hands. **E**	The gerbil eats seeds. **E** The gerbil is hungry. **C**

11

If the Shoe Fits

Read each cause statement.
Find a shoe with the matching effect.
Write the number of the cause on the shoe.

Cause Statements

1. Pip loves shopping for shoes once a week.
2. Pip doesn't like to spend a lot of money on shoes.
3. All the shoes at Gino's Shoe Store are on sale.
4. Her sneakers are old and worn out.
5. She takes tap dancing lessons.
6. Pip is going to the beach next week.
7. Pip needs help trying on shoes.
8. Gino is happy to help Pip.
9. Pip has so many choices.
10. Gino says, "If the shoe fits, buy it."

____ She only buys shoes on sale.

____ She would love a pair of sandals.

____ Pip needs a new pair of sneakers.

____ She can't make up her mind.

____ Pip buys 12 pairs of shoes.

____ He brings her a dozen pairs of shoes to try on.

____ Pip wants a pair of tap shoes.

____ She shops for shoes every Sunday.

____ She asks Gino for some help.

____ She shops at Gino's Shoe Store.

Good Pets

1. Cut apart the cards below.
2. Divide a sheet of paper into three sections and glue a heading card at the top of each section.
3. Sort the cards. Glue them in place.

For Every Learner™: Reading & Vocabulary • ©The Mailbox® Books • TEC61187 • Key p. 77

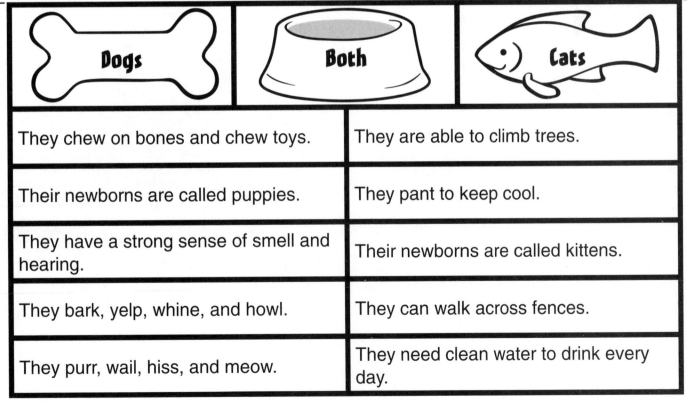

Dogs	Both	Cats
They chew on bones and chew toys.		They are able to climb trees.
Their newborns are called puppies.		They pant to keep cool.
They have a strong sense of smell and hearing.		Their newborns are called kittens.
They bark, yelp, whine, and howl.		They can walk across fences.
They purr, wail, hiss, and meow.		They need clean water to drink every day.

Lounging Lizards

Color the **same** 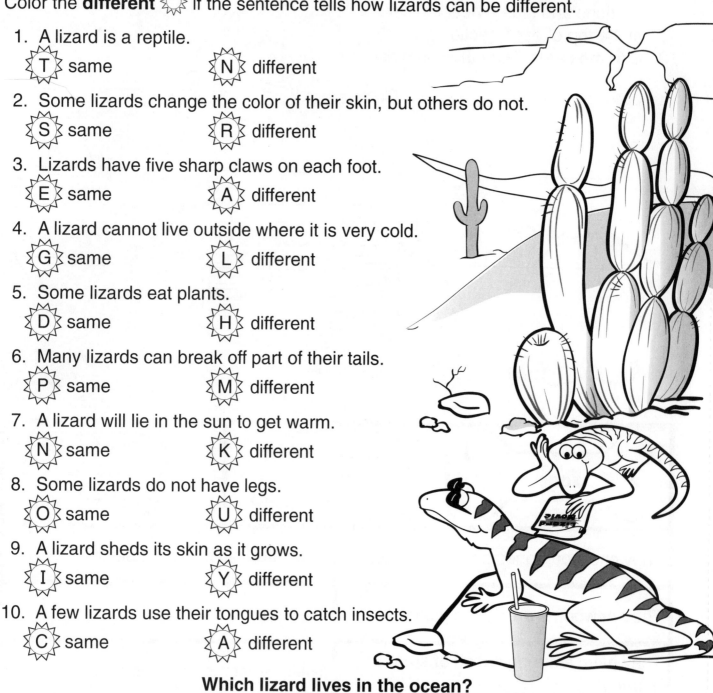 if the sentence tells how all lizards are the same.
Color the **different** if the sentence tells how lizards can be different.

1. A lizard is a reptile.
   T same   **N** different

2. Some lizards change the color of their skin, but others do not.
   S same   **R** different

3. Lizards have five sharp claws on each foot.
   E same   **A** different

4. A lizard cannot live outside where it is very cold.
   G same   **L** different

5. Some lizards eat plants.
   D same   **H** different

6. Many lizards can break off part of their tails.
   P same   **M** different

7. A lizard will lie in the sun to get warm.
   N same   **K** different

8. Some lizards do not have legs.
   O same   **U** different

9. A lizard sheds its skin as it grows.
   I same   **Y** different

10. A few lizards use their tongues to catch insects.
    C same   **A** different

Which lizard lives in the ocean?

To find out, write each colored letter from above on its matching numbered line or lines below.

___ ___ ___   ___ ___ ___ ___ ___ ___   ___ ___ ___ ___ ___ ___
 1   5   3   6 10   2   9   7   3   9   4   8 10   7 10

For Every Learner™: Reading & Vocabulary • ©The Mailbox® Books • TEC61187 • Key p. 77

Remarkable Reptiles

(Pages 15 and 16)

1. Read the paragraphs below.
2. Complete the graphic organizer on your other page.
   - Use the boxes in the middle to write about both animals.
   - Use the boxes on the left to write about alligators.
   - Use the boxes on the right to write about crocodiles.

Alligator or Crocodile

Alligators and crocodiles belong to a group of reptiles called crocodilians. They are cold-blooded animals. Alligators and crocodiles live on land and in water. Their short legs help them walk on land. They use their long tails to swim in water. They eat all kinds of small animals, such as fish, birds, and turtles.

There are many differences between alligators and crocodiles. An alligator's snout is round and wide. A crocodile has a pointed, narrow snout. When an alligator's mouth is closed, its lower jaw's teeth cannot be seen. The crocodile's lower teeth can be seen even when its mouth is closed. A crocodile's jaw is not as strong as an alligator's jaw. Crocodiles swallow their food whole. Alligators sometimes drag their food underwater and then tear it to pieces.

Alligators and crocodiles are truly two of nature's most powerful reptiles.

Name

Remarkable Reptiles

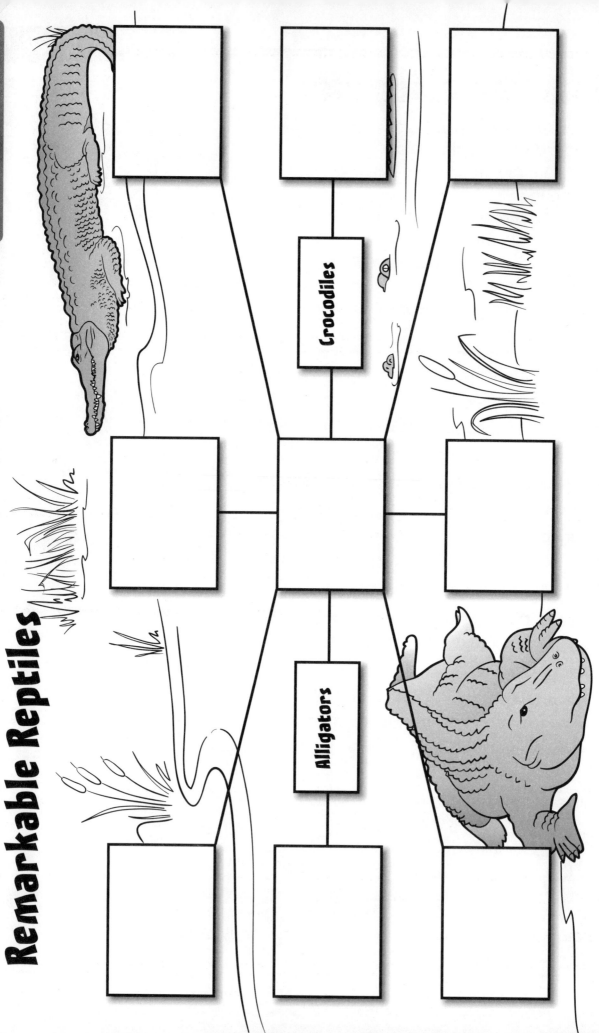

Crocodiles

Alligators

For Every Learner™: *Reading & Vocabulary* • ©The Mailbox® Books • TEC61187 • Key p. 77

Note to the teacher: Use with "Remarkable Reptiles" on page 15.

16

Nuts About Squirrels

1. Cut apart the word and sentence cards below.
2. Read a sentence and think about the meaning of the underlined word.
3. Find the word that can take the place of the underlined word.
4. Glue the matching cards on another sheet of paper.
5. Repeat with the other cards.

Sierra

For Every Learner™: Reading & Vocabulary • ©The Mailbox® Books • TEC61187 • Key p. 77

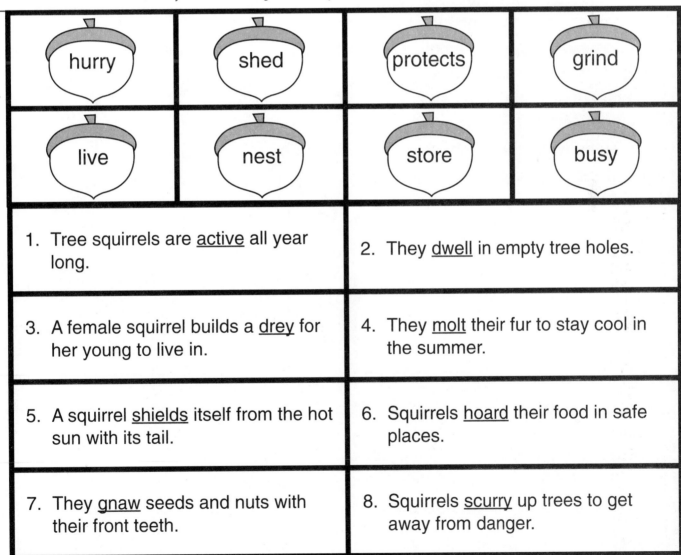

hurry	shed	protects	grind
live	nest	store	busy

1. Tree squirrels are <u>active</u> all year long.	2. They <u>dwell</u> in empty tree holes.
3. A female squirrel builds a <u>drey</u> for her young to live in.	4. They <u>molt</u> their fur to stay cool in the summer.
5. A squirrel <u>shields</u> itself from the hot sun with its tail.	6. Squirrels <u>hoard</u> their food in safe places.
7. They <u>gnaw</u> seeds and nuts with their front teeth.	8. Squirrels <u>scurry</u> up trees to get away from danger.

Kangaroos Keep Cool

Read the passage.
Write each boldfaced word next to its meaning.

Red Kangaroos

Red kangaroos live in hot, dry places. They have to find ways to stay cool in such harsh **habitats.**

Red kangaroos tend to be **nocturnal.** They search for food at night when it is cooler. They rest during the day.

Red kangaroos can dig a **hollow** to lie in. This is another way they keep their bodies cool in **scorching** weather. The hole helps to shield the kangaroos from the sun's heat.

How else do red kangaroos stay cool? They lick the hair on their arms. When the **moisture** from their arms **evaporates,** it removes heat from their bodies. This makes kangaroos feel cooler. Also, kangaroos **sweat** as they move. They **pant** through their mouths when they stop moving. The quick breaths cool the kangaroos.

These kangaroos sure know how to beat the heat!

1. breathe fast _____

2. environments _____

3. hole in the ground _____

4. disappears _____

5. active at night _____

6. tiny water drops _____

7. very hot _____

8. release beads of water from the body _____

Buzzing Beehive

(Pages 19 and 20)

1. Cut apart the word cards below.
2. Read each sentence on your other page.
3. Underline the clue words in each sentence that help you understand the meaning of the boldfaced word or words.
4. Glue each word card atop the • of its matching sentence.

For Every Learner™: Reading & Vocabulary • ©The Mailbox® Books • TEC61187 • Key p. 77

fix	scent	queen
release	search	attracted
attack	group	guard
help	supply	warn

Buzzing Beehive

1. Thousands of honeybees live and work within a **colony.**

2. Only one **female bee** in the hive lays eggs.

3. Worker bees build the hive and **repair** any cracks.

4. Worker bees also **defend** the hive's entrance from enemies.

5. A guard bee can smell the **odor** of a bee from another hive.

6. Guard bees will **swarm** a bear that may harm the hive.

7. Hungry bears are **lured** to the honey inside a beehive.

8. The guard bees **alert** the other bees of any danger.

9. Guard bees **emit** a special scent that smells like bananas.

10. The other bees **aid** the guard bees if the hive is invaded.

11. A scout bee's job is to **hunt** for food and find new hives.

12. Flowers **provide** bees with the food they need.

For Every Learner™: *Reading & Vocabulary* • ©The Mailbox® Books • TEC61187 • Key p. 77

Get in Line!

(Pages 21 and 22)

1. Cut apart the cards below.
2. Read the sentences on your other page.
3. Glue each card next to its matching sentences.

For Every Learner™: Reading & Vocabulary • ©The Mailbox® Books • TEC61187 • Key p. 77

bat	bee
owl	shark
snake	toad

Get in Line!

1. It has wings.
   It flies.
   It is an insect.

2. It breathes with gills.
   It lives in water.
   It is a fish.

3. It has fur.
   Its babies feed on mother's milk.
   It is a mammal.

4. It has feathers and wings.
   It hatches from an egg.
   It is a bird.

5. Its skin does not have scales.
   It spends part of its life on land and part of its
      life in water.
   It is an amphibian.

6. Its skin has scales.
   It is cold-blooded.
   It is a reptile.

Under the Sea

Read each set of sentences.
Draw a ✔ next to the sentence that is supported
   by the other sentences.

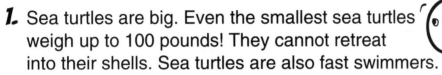

1. Sea turtles are big. Even the smallest sea turtles
weigh up to 100 pounds! They cannot retreat
into their shells. Sea turtles are also fast swimmers.
___ Sea turtles use their size and fast swimming to
   stay safe.
___ Sea turtles cannot defend themselves.

2. A starfish is also called a sea star. Most starfish have five arms. This makes
them look like five-pointed stars. But starfish are not fish. They are part of a
group of sea animals called echinoderms.
___ Starfish are sea animals.
___ Starfish get their name based on how they look.

3. A female lobster may only produce eggs every other year. When she does,
she has between 3,000 and 100,000 eggs. An adult lobster can live 15 years
or longer, but most do not live that long. They end up as prey to other animals
and to people.
___ A female lobster has a lot of eggs to increase the chances of having
   offspring that will become adults.
___ A female lobster has a lot of eggs because she can live a long time.

4. Even though it lives in water, a whale is a mammal,
not a fish. It does not use gills to breathe. It uses its
lungs. A whale has to swim to the surface of the water
to take in air. Luckily, a whale can hold its breath. One
kind of whale can hold its breath for almost two hours!
___ One way a whale is different from a fish is how it
   breathes.
___ Fish and whales live in water.

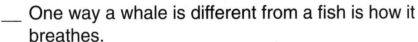

Name

"Sssssnakes"

Read each paragraph.
Complete the chart.

Paragraph	+ Related Facts I Already Knew =	My Conclusion
Snakes live almost all over the world. Some are ground dwellers, and some live underground. Others live in water. There are not many places where snakes don't live. They cannot survive in places where the ground is frozen all year.		
Snakes are reptiles. Reptiles are cold-blooded. This means the temperature of a snake's body is about the same as the temperature outside. If a snake needs to get warm, it might lie in the sun. If it needs to cool down, it might rest in the shade.		
Some people do not like snakes. They think they are all dangerous. But snakes are helpful animals. They help farmers by eating pesky mice and rats. Snakes' venom is used in some medicines.		

Fishy Facts

(Pages 25 and 26)

1. Cut apart the cards below.
2. Read the cards and sort them on your other page.
3. Glue the cards in place.

For Every Learner™: Reading & Vocabulary • ©The Mailbox® Books • TEC61187 • Key p. 78

Fish tanks are easy to care for.	Fish tanks come in different shapes and sizes.	An aquarist is a person who keeps a fish tank.	Colorful gravel makes a fish tank look pretty.
Pet stores sell all sorts of fish.	Fish are fun pets to watch.	There are many different kinds of fish.	Most fish should be fed at least once a day.
Guppies are one type of pet fish.	Tropical fish tanks need to be heated.	Goldfish are the best kind of pet fish.	An aquarium is a container for fish.
	Plants can give fish homes and food.	Fish live in either freshwater or saltwater.	

Fishy Facts

Facts

Opinions

For Every Learner™: Reading & Vocabulary • ©The Mailbox® Books • TEC61187 • Key p. 78

Note to the teacher: Use with "Fishy Facts" on page 25.

X Marks the Spot

Cut apart the cards below.
Match each card to a fact or an opinion
 sentence to make a map of the island.
Glue each card to its •.

•	•	•
The pirate is greedy.	The pirate looks for buried treasure.	He uses a map to find the treasure.
•	•	•
The island is beautiful.	His crew is very helpful.	The treasure chest is filled with gold coins.
•	•	•
The pirate searches the island.	Treasure hunts are fun!	The pirate digs in the sand with a shovel.

For Every Learner™: Reading & Vocabulary • ©The Mailbox® Books • TEC61187 • Key p. 78

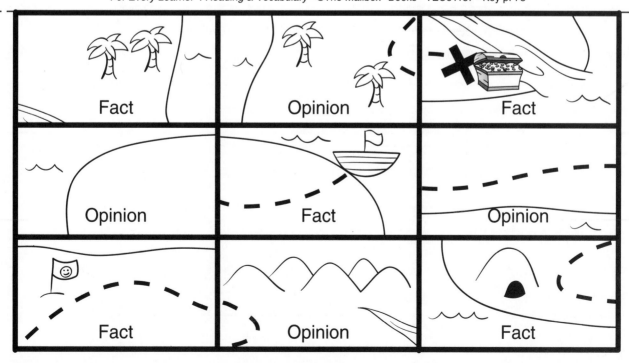

Fact	Opinion	Fact
Opinion	Fact	Opinion
Fact	Opinion	Fact

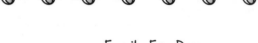
Just the Facts, Please!

Read the sentences on the notepad.
Decide whether each sentence is a fact or an opinion.
Color each circle by the code.

Color Code
fact = green
opinion = yellow

Family Fun Day

1. City leaders planned a family fun day at Elm Park.
2. Over 500 families came to the free event.
3. The weather was perfect!
4. There were rides, games, and contests.
5. Children loved the face-painting booth.
6. Hot dogs, cupcakes, and fresh lemonade were served.
7. The band's music was great.
8. It was a fun day.

Write the number of each opinion sentence in a square below.
Rewrite each sentence to make it a fact.

☐ _____

☐ _____

☐ _____

☐ _____

For Every Learner™: Reading & Vocabulary • ©The Mailbox® Books • TEC61187 • Key p. 78

The Nose Knows!

1. Cut apart the cards below.
2. Match each pair of homophones.
3. Glue the cards on another sheet of paper.

For Every Learner™: Reading & Vocabulary • ©The Mailbox® Books • TEC61187 • Key p. 78

some	hear	write	sew
so	our	wear	sum
brake	nose	here	break
piece	right	hour	maid
made	where	knows	peace

Dancing Diva

Color the word that best completes each sentence.

	T	A
1. Shannon is so ____!	bored	board
2. She cannot ____ for dance class!	**F** wait	**B** weight
3. She knows just what she wants to ____ to class.	**A** where	**I** wear
4. First, she puts on a ____ of slippers.	**E** pair	**A** pear
5. Then she slides a tutu around her ____	**L** waste	**S** waist
6. After that, she ties her ____ back in a bow.	**G** hair	**E** hare
7. She also adds a ____.	**R** flour	**T** flower
8. Once she is dressed, Shannon grabs ____ water bottles.	**L** two	**I** too
9. "____," she says.	**N** Their	**H** There
10. "Now I'm ready for a ____ of dancing! Too 'baa-d' it's not until tomorrow!"	**A** knight	**U** night

What do you call a dancing sheep?
To solve the riddle, write each uncolored letter from above in order on the lines below.

___ " ___ ___ - ___ ___ ___ ___ ___ ___ "

Rock-and-Roll Rats

(Pages 31 and 32)

Directions for two players:

1. Cut apart the key and spinner below.
2. Cut apart the cards on your other page. Lay the cards faceup on the playing surface.
3. When it's your turn, use a paper clip and pencil to spin the spinner. Choose a game card that matches the spin. If a match cannot be made, your turn is over.
4. Have your partner use the key to check your answer. If you are correct, keep the card. If not, return the card.
5. Play until all the cards are taken. The player with more cards wins.

For Every Learner™: Reading & Vocabulary • ©The Mailbox® Books • TEC61187

Answer Key

1. incorrect
2. correct
3. incorrect
4. correct
5. correct
6. incorrect
7. correct
8. correct
9. correct
10. incorrect
11. correct
12. incorrect
13. incorrect
14. incorrect
15. correct

Spinner

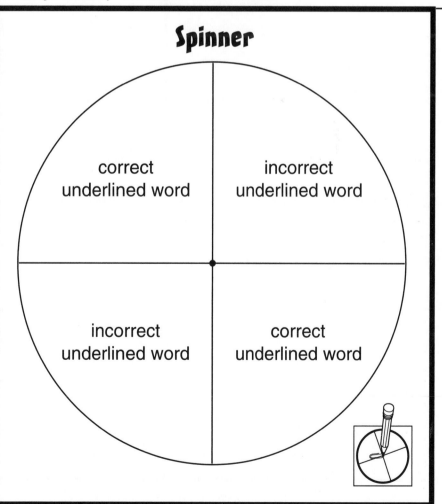

correct underlined word

incorrect underlined word

incorrect underlined word

correct underlined word

Rock-and-Roll Rats

3. They're music can get really loud!

6. Sometimes the band travels on the rode.

9. Good weather or bad, the band is ready to play.

12. They will perform every night this weak.

15. After each show, the lead singer likes to drink a cup of tea.

2. They would play every day if they could.

5. The music can be heard for miles.

8. Once they took a boat called a ferry to get across a river.

11. They have only been together for three months.

14. The lead singer will merry next month.

1. The banned loves to play music!

4. The band never misses a beat.

7. Other times they travel by plane.

10. I might have guest that they have played together for years!

13. Sometimes the band members wear matching close.

For Every Learner™: Reading & Vocabulary • ©The Mailbox® Books • TEC61187

32 **Note to the teacher:** Use with "Rock-and-Roll Rats" on page 31.

Time for a Change

(Pages 33 and 34)

1. Cut apart the cards below.
2. Place the cards under the matching life cycle on your other page.
3. Glue the cards in place.

For Every Learner™: *Reading & Vocabulary* • ©The Mailbox® Books • TEC61187 • Key p. 78

An adult ladybug lays eggs.	A butterfly is an egg before it is a caterpillar.
A ladybug goes through four stages of life.	A butterfly goes through four stages of life.
A butterfly is a caterpillar before it forms a chrysalis.	A ladybug in the larval stage is called a grub.

Time for a Change

Life Cycle of a Butterfly

Egg

A butterfly starts its life as an egg.

Larva

A caterpillar comes from the egg.

Pupa

The caterpillar forms a shell called a chrysalis.

Adult

A butterfly comes from the chrysalis and may soon lay eggs.

Life Cycle of a Ladybug

Egg

A ladybug starts life as an egg.

Larva

It is also called a grub. It sheds its outer covering many times.

Pupa

The grub almost looks like an adult ladybug. It is softer and has a different color.

Adult

A ladybug has a short life as an adult. It mates quickly.

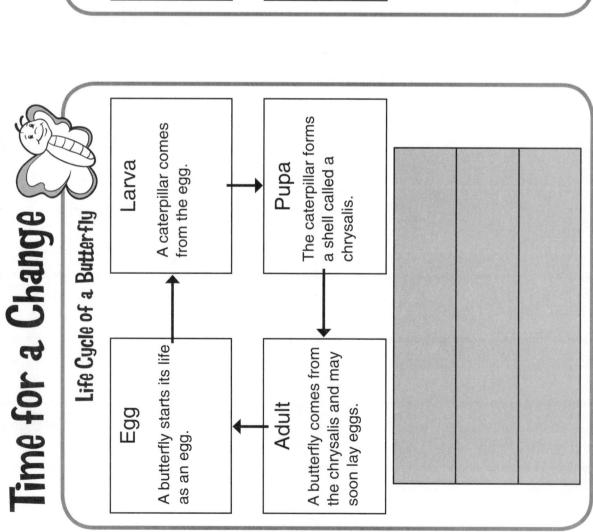

For Every Learner™: *Reading & Vocabulary* • ©The Mailbox® Books • TEC61187 • Key p. 78

Note to the teacher: Use with "Time for a Change" on page 33.

What Goes Up...

Read the flowchart.
Answer each question by circling the best answer.

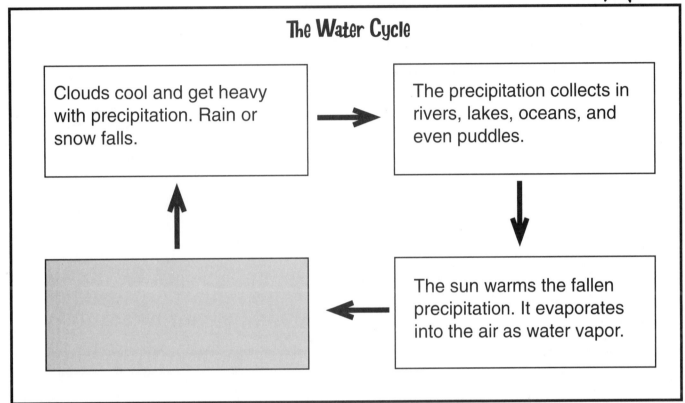

The Water Cycle

Clouds cool and get heavy with precipitation. Rain or snow falls.

→

The precipitation collects in rivers, lakes, oceans, and even puddles.

↓

The sun warms the fallen precipitation. It evaporates into the air as water vapor.

←

1. What is precipitation?
   rain or snow   pretend weather

2. What happens after clouds get heavy with precipitation?
   puddles form   rain or snow falls from them

3. Where does precipitation collect before it evaporates?
   in clouds   in lakes

4. What helps the fallen precipitation evaporate?
   sun   precipitation

5. Which of these belongs in the empty rectangle?
   Water vapor condenses into clouds.   Water vapor falls back to the earth.

Budding Readers

1. Read the cards below and then cut them out.
2. Arrange the small cards to make a flowchart on another sheet of paper.
3. Glue the cards in place.
4. Write three sentences about the flowchart. Use the sentence starters to help you.
5. Glue the sentence starters card on the back of your paper.

HOW A SEED GROWS

From Seed to Flower

A Plant Life Cycle

Flora

For Every Learner™: Reading & Vocabulary • ©The Mailbox® Books • TEC61187 • Key p. 78

When the seed gets the right amount of sun and water, it grows a stem and roots. 	A flowering plant starts as a seed. The seed grows in soil. 	**Sentence Starters** Before a seed grows a stem and roots, Before seeds grow at the base of the flowers, Before growing flowers, a plant After a seed gets sun and water, After a seed grows a stem and roots, After the plant grows leaves and flowers,
Flowers get pollinated by insects, animals, and even the wind. Seeds grow at the base of the flowers.	The plant grows leaves and flowers. 	

Saint Bernard Sort

(Pages 37 and 38)

1. Cut apart the cards below.
2. Put a main idea card on each doghouse on your other page.
3. Put each supporting detail below its main idea.
4. Glue the cards in place.

For Every Learner™: Reading & Vocabulary • ©The Mailbox® Books • TEC61187 • Key p. 78

main idea **How Well Dogs See**	main idea **How Well Dogs Hear**
Dogs are able to see moving objects very well.	Faraway objects look blurry to dogs.
Dogs hear high-pitched sounds that humans do not.	Dogs hear four times better than humans.
Dogs cannot see all the colors that humans see.	Dogs can see well in dim light.
Some dogs can hear storms that are many miles away.	Dogs may know the sounds of their owners' cars.

Saint Bernard Sort

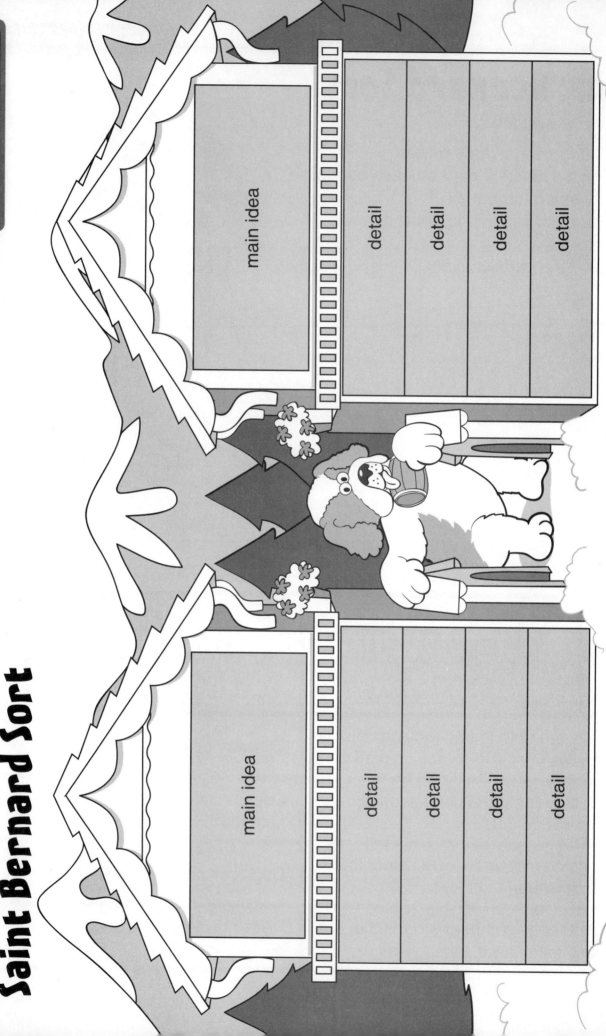

main idea

detail

detail

detail

detail

main idea

detail

detail

detail

detail

For Every Learner™: *Reading & Vocabulary* • ©The Mailbox® Books • TEC61187 • Key p. 78

Note to the teacher: Use with "Saint Bernard Sort" on page 37.

Hockey Time

Read each set of sentences.
Underline the main idea.
Cross out the sentence that does not support the main idea.

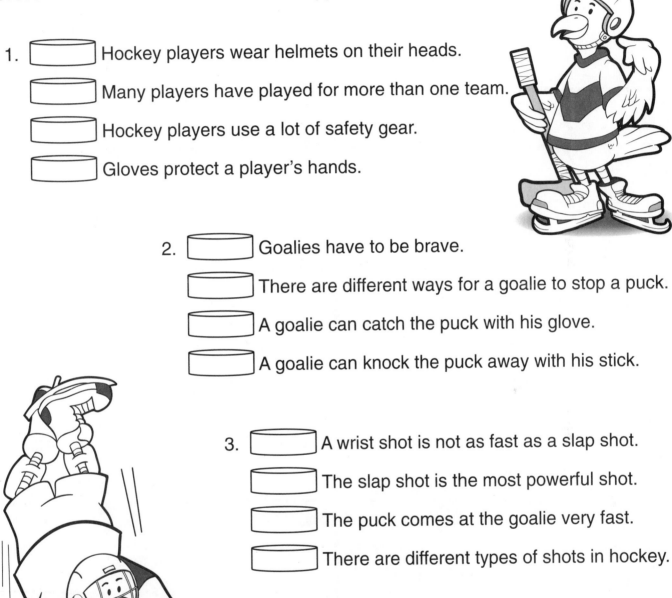

1. ⬭ Hockey players wear helmets on their heads.

   ⬭ Many players have played for more than one team.

   ⬭ Hockey players use a lot of safety gear.

   ⬭ Gloves protect a player's hands.

2. ⬭ Goalies have to be brave.

   ⬭ There are different ways for a goalie to stop a puck.

   ⬭ A goalie can catch the puck with his glove.

   ⬭ A goalie can knock the puck away with his stick.

3. ⬭ A wrist shot is not as fast as a slap shot.

   ⬭ The slap shot is the most powerful shot.

   ⬭ The puck comes at the goalie very fast.

   ⬭ There are different types of shots in hockey.

4. ⬭ Hockey is played in different countries.

   ⬭ The United States hockey team won a gold medal in 1980.

   ⬭ The United States has many hockey teams.

   ⬭ Canada is known for its hockey teams.

Under the Big Top

1. Cut out the cards below.
2. Sort the cards into two sets of supporting details.
3. Glue each set to another sheet of paper.
4. Write a main idea above each set.

Chimps ride on bicycles
around the ring.

Circus clowns ride
unicycles.

Some circus clowns
walk on stilts.

Amazing clowns juggle
balls and pins.

Elephants walk in a line with
their tails and trunks hooked.

Tigers jump through
fire hoops.

Sometimes dogs jump rope
at the circus.

Circus clowns all squeeze
into a small car.

Roy the Groundskeeper

Circle the letter to show the correct meaning of the underlined word.

1. Roy grabbed a <u>rake</u> and his lawn mower.
   S. tool for gathering grass or leaves   B. gather grass or leaves with a tool

2. He had to work in his <u>yard</u>.
   E. unit of length equal to three feet   I. grassy area around a house

3. First, Roy picked up the <u>sticks</u> under the tree.
   M. pokes with a pointed object   K. dry, broken twigs

4. Next, he raked all the <u>leaves</u> off the ground.
   R. flat, usuallly green parts of a tree   F. goes away

5. Then Roy <u>cut</u> the grass.
   T. trimmed with a sharp tool   W. injury caused by a sharp object

6. He put his rake and lawn mower in the <u>shed</u>.
   C. get rid of   N. storage building

7. Roy <u>saw</u> that his yard was beautiful.
   H. noticed   Y. tool used for cutting

8. So he took a <u>rest</u> under a tree.
   A. something left over   O. nap

How do you get a rhinoceros's attention?

To solve the riddle, write each circled
letter from above on its matching numbered
line or lines below.

__ __ __ __   __ __ __   __ __ __ __
7 8 6 3   2 5 1   7 8 4 6

Grand Slam

1. Cut apart the sentence and word cards below.
2. Match each pair of sentences with a word that completes both of them.
3. Glue the matching cards on another sheet of paper.

For Every Learner™: Reading & Vocabulary • ©The Mailbox® Books • TEC61187 • Key p. 79

The _____ keeps us cool. Tim is a _____ of baseball.	We saw a ball game at the _____. He will _____ the car in the lot.
She fills the _____ with water. The _____ threw a fastball.	Who wants to _____ baseball? The class put on a _____.
The skater will _____ across the ice. Jen slid down the _____.	Kim will _____ the bat. Will you push me on the _____?
Our soccer _____ is the best. My dad will _____ the team.	The money is kept in a _____. The runner was _____ at first base.
Mom mixed the cake _____. The last _____ hit a home run.	Sam won a goldfish at the _____. The team played a _____ game.

fan	swing	park	fair	slide
pitcher	safe	batter	play	coach

It's a Toss-Up

(Pages 43 and 44)

Directions for two players:

1. Cut apart the cards below and stack them facedown.
2. When it's your turn, take the top card.
3. Read the definitions. Write on the crossword puzzle the word that matches both definitions. If the word is not known, return the card to the bottom of the stack.
4. Use a dictionary to verify the answer. If correct, keep the card. If incorrect, return the card to the bottom of the stack and erase the answer.
5. Take turns in this manner. The player with more cards wins.

For Every Learner™: Reading & Vocabulary • ©The Mailbox® Books • TEC61187 • Key p. 79

---

1 Across
1. unit of length equal to 12 inches
2. body part attached to the leg

1 Down
1. form a knot or bow
2. when a game ends with an equal score

2 Across
1. long, thin tool for hitting
2. win or defeat

2 Down
1. keep in view
2. timepiece worn on the wrist

3 Across
1. now, today
2. gift

3 Down
1. unit of weight equal to 16 ounces
2. strike again and again

4 Across
1. very small piece
2. took a bite

4 Down
1. direct someone's attention
2. sharp tip

5 Across
1. make the equal of
2. used to start a fire

5 Down
1. small bird with a forked tail
2. take into the stomach through the mouth

6 Across
1. cargo that is moved
2. fill a container

6 Down
1. moved upward
2. flower

7 Across
1. bread made crisp by heat
2. to warm

7 Down
1. having little weight
2. not a dark color

8 Across
1. rhythm
2. tired, exhausted

8 Down
1. roll a ball to knock over objects
2. deep dish

9 Across
1. one who counts
2. flat surface for serving food

9 Down
1. fictional tale
2. one floor level of a building

It's a Toss-Up

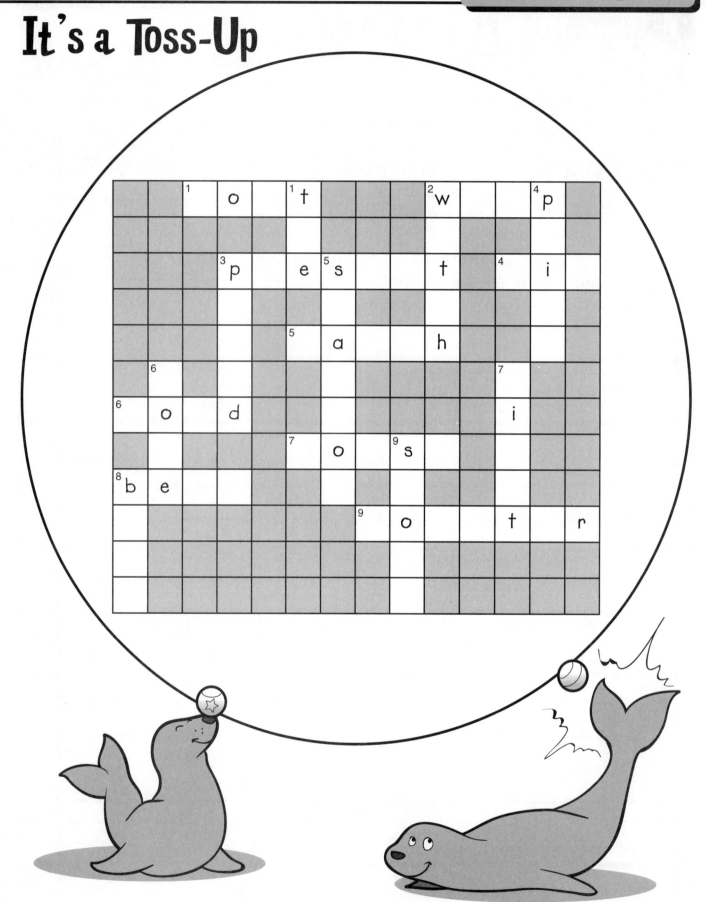

For Every Learner™: Reading & Vocabulary • ©The Mailbox® Books • TEC61187 • Key p. 79

44   **Note to the teacher:** Use with "It's a Toss-Up" on page 43.

A Bunch of Belongings

1. Underline the owner in each phrase.
2. Cut apart the cards.
3. Sort the cards by owner: singular or plural.
4. Glue both sets to another sheet of paper. Label each set with its title.

Gordon

Singular   Plural

For Every Learner™: Reading & Vocabulary • ©The Mailbox® Books • TEC61187 • Key p. 79

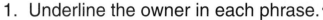

hen's egg	frogs' pond
kangaroo's pouch	crab's shell
bats' cave	bears' den
goats' mountain	turkey's wattle
lion's mane	cows' barn

Visiting School

(Pages 46 and 47)

1. Cut apart the cards below.
2. Put glue on a • on your other page.
3. Glue the card with the matching meaning onto the •.
4. Repeat with the other cards.

Visitor

For Every Learner™: Reading & Vocabulary • ©The Mailbox® Books • TEC61187 • Key p. 79

bus drivers' parking lot	class's pet	nurse's ice pack
parents' meeting	principal's office	student's homework
students' teacher	teacher's bag	teachers' lounge
		visitor's badge

Visiting School

homework that belongs to a student

lounge used by teachers

pet that belongs to a class

bag that belongs to a teacher

parking lot used by bus drivers

office used by the principal

teacher who belongs to students

meeting for parents

badge that belongs to a visitor

ice pack that belongs to a nurse

Visitor

Note to the teacher: Use with "Visiting School" on page 46.

Running Behind

Circle the letter of the words that best replace the underlined words.

1. Eli is going on a trip to <u>the summer home belonging to his aunt</u>.
   H. his aunt's summer home   L. his aunts' summer home

2. <u>The ticket belonging to Eli</u> states that he has to be on the plane at 4:00.
   F. Eli's ticket   J. Elis' ticket

3. Eli decides to take a swim in <u>the pool belonging to his neighbors</u> before he leaves for the airport.
   D. his neighbor's pool   S. his neighbors' pool

4. First, he uses <u>the snorkel belonging to Ed</u>.
   R. Ed's snorkel   P. Eds' snorkel

5. Then he uses <u>the raft belonging to Ellen</u>.
   G. Ellen's raft   M. Ellens' raft

6. He checks <u>the watch belonging to his brother</u> and sees that it is 3:45!
   E. his brother's watch   V. his brothers' watch

7. He stomps through <u>the garden belonging to his mother</u> as he runs home.
   T. his mother's garden   C. his mothers' garden

8. Then he grabs <u>the snack belonging to his sisters</u> and wolfs it down.
   W. his sister's snack   I. his sisters' snack

9. Eli jumps over <u>the luggage belonging to his parents</u> and races down the hall.
   B. his parent's luggage   O. his parents' luggage

10. Eli makes a mad dash to the <u>airport belonging to the city</u>.
    N. city's airport   A. citys' airport

11. He passes the <u>park belonging to the children</u> along the way.
    K. children's park   G. childrens' park

12. As he passes the <u>bake sale belonging to the singers</u>, he recalls something very important and has to turn back!
    X. singer's bake sale   U. singers' bake sale

Why was Eli the elephant late for the plane?

To solve the riddle, write each circled letter from above on its matching numbered line or lines below.

___ ___   ___ ___ ___ ___ ___ ___   ___ ___ ___   ___ ___ ___ ___ ___.
1 6   2 9 4 5 9 7   1 8 3   7 4 12 10 11

 For Every Learner™: Reading & Vocabulary • ©The Mailbox® Books • TEC61187 • Key p. 79

Busy Beaver

Cut apart the cards below.
Read each definition.
Match a prefix card to a base word card
  to make the matching word.
Glue the cards in place.

re- = again
pre- = before
dis- = not or opposite of
un- = not

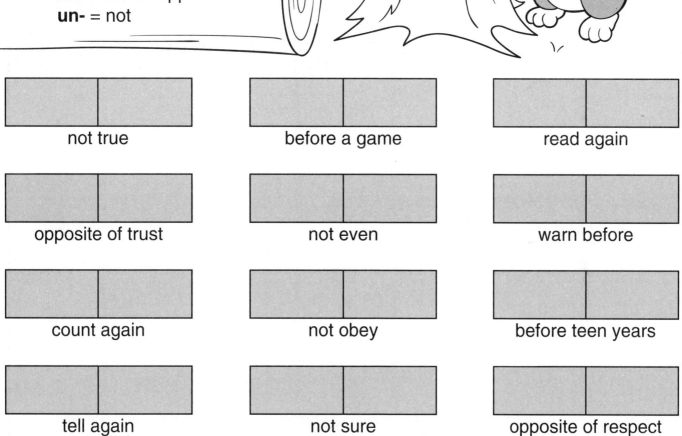

not true

before a game

read again

opposite of trust

not even

warn before

count again

not obey

before teen years

tell again

not sure

opposite of respect

For Every Learner™: Reading & Vocabulary • ©The Mailbox® Books • TEC61187 • Key p. 79

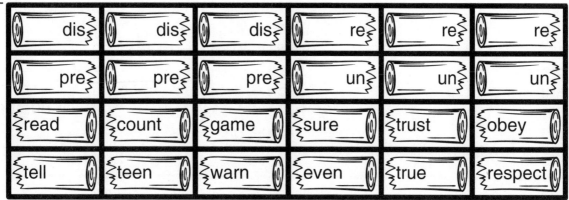

dis	dis	dis	re	re	re
pre	pre	pre	un	un	un
read	count	game	sure	trust	obey
tell	teen	warn	even	true	respect

Hop On Over

(Pages 50 and 51)

Directions for two players:

1. Cut apart the cards and key below. Then cut apart the gameboards on your other page.
2. Stack the cards facedown and take a gameboard. Set the key aside.
3. When it's your turn, take a card and read the prefix with each word on your gameboard until you make a match. Place the card on top of the word and have your partner check the answer key. If no match can be made, return the card to the bottom of the stack.
4. The first player to fill his path wins.

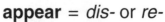

pre-	pre-	un-	un-	re-	re-	Take **2** cards.
pre-	pre-	un-	un-	re-	re-	Take **2** cards.
pre-	pre-	un-	un-	re-	re-	Take **2** cards.
dis-	un-	un-	un-	re-	re-	re-
dis-	dis-	dis-	dis-	dis-	dis-	re-

Answer Key

agree = *dis-*

build = *re-* or *un-*

color = *dis-* or *re-*

fold = *re-* or *un-*

locate = *dis-* or *re-*

order = *dis-, pre-,* or *re-*

start = *re-*

writing = *pre-* or *re-*

appear = *dis-* or *re-*

clear = *pre-* or *un-*

cover = *dis-, re-,* or *un-*

load = *pre-, re-,* or *un-*

lock = *re-* or *un-*

school = *pre-* or *re-*

tie = *un-* or *re-*

Prefixes: *dis-, pre-, re-, un-*

Hop On Over

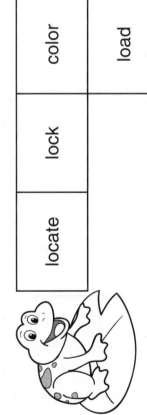

clear	color	writing
		cover
appear	load	school
start	tie	
build	fold	agree
		order
		lock
		locate

For Every Learner™: Reading & Vocabulary • ©The Mailbox® Books • TEC61187

Prefixes: *dis-, pre-, re-, un-*

Hop On Over

locate	lock	color
		load
order	agree	start
cover	build	
clear	appear	fold
	school	writing
		tie

For Every Learner™: Reading & Vocabulary • ©The Mailbox® Books • TEC61187

Note to the teacher: Use with "Hop On Over" on page 50.

51

Sort It Out!

1. Cut apart the prefix and base word cards below.
2. Glue the prefix cards across the top of another sheet of paper.
3. Under each prefix, put the base word cards that can be added to the prefix to make real words.
4. Glue the cards in place.

For Every Learner™: Reading & Vocabulary • ©The Mailbox® Books • TEC61187 • Key p. 79

dis-	pre-	re-	un-	re- pre-	dis- un-	un- re- pre-
try	paid	paint	like	copy	number	plan
heat	call	trace	season	lucky	able	happy
certain	fair	honest	aware	agree	belief	wash
test	easy	loyal	caution	cut	wrap	bake

Catch of the Day

(Pages 53 and 54)
Directions for two players:

1. Cut apart the cards and key below. Shuffle the cards and stack them facedown. Set the key aside.
2. Place a game marker on Start on your other page.
3. Read the story and follow the directions to play.

For Every Learner™: Reading & Vocabulary • ©The Mailbox® Books • TEC61187

---

1. What is Pete's job on the fishing boat? **If correct, move ahead 1 space.**	**2.** What is the name of Pete's boat? **If correct, move ahead 1 space.**	**3.** On which ocean do Pete and his crew sail? **If correct, move ahead 1 space.**
4. How many days does the crew spend fishing? **If correct, move ahead 2 spaces.**	**5.** When does Pete turn off the boat motor? **If correct, move ahead 3 spaces.**	**6.** What keeps the boat from floating away? **If correct, move ahead 1 space.**
7. Why does the crew dive off the boat? **If correct, move ahead 2 spaces.**	**8.** With what do Pete and his crew fill their pouches? **If correct, move ahead 2 spaces.**	**9.** Where does the crew store the fish? **If correct, move ahead 2 spaces.**
10. When do Pete and his crew sail back to the docks? **If correct, move ahead 2 spaces**	**11.** Why do Pete and his crew sail back to the docks? **If correct, move ahead 3 spaces.**	**12.** How does Pete feel about his crew and their work? **If correct, move ahead 2 spaces.**

Answer Key

1. captain
2. *Sea More*
3. Atlantic Ocean
4. three days
5. when he finds the best spot to fish
6. a heavy anchor

7. to start fishing
8. dozens of fish
9. in tanks
10. after they catch plenty of fish
11. to sell fish
12. proud

Catch of the Day

Pelican Pete

Pete is the captain of a large fishing boat named *Sea More.* He and his crew travel for miles over the Atlantic Ocean in search of fish. They spend three days fishing on the ocean. Pete turns off the boat's motor when he finds the best spot to fish. Then his crew lowers a heavy anchor into the deep water. It keeps the boat from floating away. They dive off the side of the boat and start to fish. Each crew member fills his pouch with dozens of fish. They bring the fish back to the boat and store the fish in tanks. After they catch plenty of fish, Pete and his crew sail back to the docks to sell the fish. They sell the fresh fish to others. Pete is proud of his crew and their work.

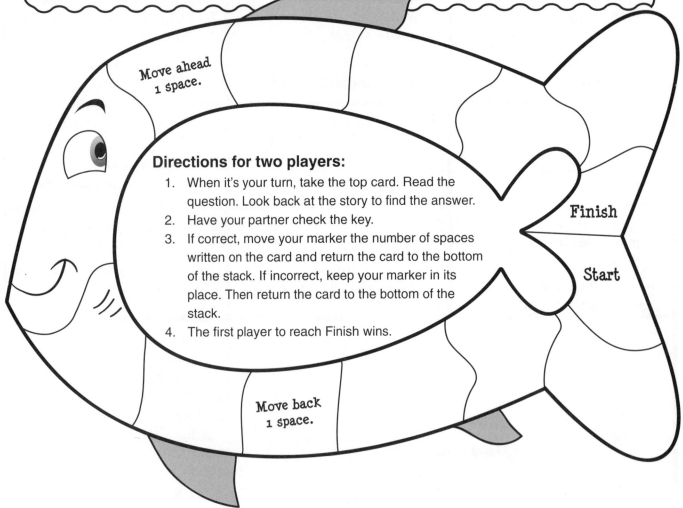

Move ahead 1 space.

Directions for two players:

1. When it's your turn, take the top card. Read the question. Look back at the story to find the answer.
2. Have your partner check the key.
3. If correct, move your marker the number of spaces written on the card and return the card to the bottom of the stack. If incorrect, keep your marker in its place. Then return the card to the bottom of the stack.
4. The first player to reach Finish wins.

Finish

Start

Move back 1 space.

For Every Learner™: Reading & Vocabulary • ©The Mailbox® Books • TEC61187

Get in the Game

1. Read the story.
2. Cut apart the cards below.
3. Divide another sheet of paper into two columns.
4. Label one column "True" and the other column "False."
5. Glue each card in the matching column.

Basketball's Best

Jenna will be nine years old this summer. Her sister, Jamie, is three years older. Jamie is the tallest player on the school's basketball team. Jenna wishes she could play basketball like Jamie. Jenna wants to try out for the basketball team next year but worries that she won't make it. Jenna never learned how to play the game.

One afternoon, Jenna asks her sister to teach her how to play. The two girls go to the basketball court at the park. First, Jamie shows Jenna how to dribble the ball. Next, she teaches Jenna the correct way to pass the ball. Then they practice throwing the basketball through the hoop. Jenna learns quickly. Finally, Jamie invites Jenna to play against her in a game. Jenna beats Jamie by two points. Jamie is proud of her sister's skills. She tells Jenna that she is a very good player. Jenna smiles at Jamie and says, "I learned from the best!"

For Every Learner™: Reading & Vocabulary • ©The Mailbox® Books • TEC61187 • Key p. 79

Jamie is three years older than Jenna.	Jamie doesn't think she will make the team.	Jenna learns to play basketball at the park.
Jenna's birthday is in the summer.	Jamie wants to try out for the team.	Jenna learns the wrong way to pass.
Jamie thinks Jenna is not a very good player.	Jenna wishes to play basketball like Jamie.	Jamie scores two more points than Jenna.
Jenna teaches Jamie to play basketball.	The girls play a game of basketball.	Jenna learns how to dribble the basketball.

A "Terrrrific" Car Wash

Read the story.

Trevor owns one of the best car washes in all of Tiger City. His car wash is open Monday through Saturday from sunup to sundown. It is located on Main Street. Cars fill the street every Saturday morning. That is because Trevor takes extra good care of the cars he cleans. First, he scrubs the dirt and grime off the tires. Next, Trevor gently lathers the entire car with fresh-scented soap. Then he rinses the suds off with warm water. The car is sparkling clean, but he's not done yet. Trevor applies a special wax. He buffs the car until it shines. The cars are driven away looking brand-new, and their owners are happy. Trevor is happy too. He likes to make his customers feel good.

Answer the questions.

1. Who owns one of the best car washes in Tiger City? _____

2. On which street is the car wash located? _____

3. How many days is the car wash open? _____

4. Why do car owners choose Trevor to wash their cars? _____
   _____

5. What does Trevor do after he scrubs the tires? _____
   _____

6. What does Trevor use to rinse the soapy cars? _____
   _____

7. How do the cars look as they are driven away? _____
   _____

8. Why is Trevor happy? _____
   _____

A Snail's Pace

1. Cut apart the puzzle pieces below.
2. Glue the pieces together on another sheet of paper in the order in which the events happened.

For Every Learner™: *Reading & Vocabulary* • ©The Mailbox® Books • TEC61187 • Key p. 79

5. Later,	she climbed up a flower stem.
6. Finally,	Sue slid across some rocks.
4. Then	she crawled over a tall fence.
2. First,	Sue went into the garden.
1. Early one morning,	she rested in the shade.
3. Next,	Sue hid under a leaf.

Bright Smile

Cut apart the sentence cards.
Glue the events onto the toothbrush in the order in which
    they happen.

| 1 |
| 2 |
| 3 |
| 4 |
| 5 |
| 6 |
| 7 |
| 8 |

As soon as Sam wakes up, he brushes his teeth.

Before Sam spits out the toothpaste, he brushes his gums.

Next, Sam squeezes toothpaste onto his toothbrush.

Sam smiles in the mirror to see his clean teeth.

Sam moves the toothbrush gently across his teeth.

First, he holds his toothbrush with one fin.

Finally, he rinses his mouth with water.

Then he puts the toothbrush in his mouth.

A Swell Retelling

(Pages 59 and 60)

1. Cut apart the cards below.
2. Number the cards in each box to show the order of the events.
3. Glue the cards in order. Then write a sentence on your other page about each picture.

For Every Learner™: Reading & Vocabulary • ©The Mailbox® Books • TEC61187 • Key p. 79

A Swell Retelling

First, _____

_____

Next, _____

_____

Then _____

_____

After that _____

_____

Finally, _____

_____

Note to the teacher: Use with "A Swell Retelling" on page 59.

Happy Endings

1. Underline the suffix in each word below.
2. Cut apart the cards.
3. Sort the cards by suffix.
4. Glue each set to another sheet of paper. Label each set with its suffix.

Bella

For Every Learner™: Reading & Vocabulary • ©The Mailbox® Books • TEC61187 • Key p. 80

breakable	loudly	movable
neatly	quickly	slowly
softly	teachable	trainable
washable	wearable	wisely

Powerful Protector

(Pages 62 and 63)

1. Cut apart the cards below.
2. Match the word on each card with its meaning on your other page.
3. When all the cards have been sorted, glue them in place.

For Every Learner™: Reading & Vocabulary • ©The Mailbox® Books • TEC61187 • Key p. 80

badly	believable
bravely	breakable
clearly	honestly
movable	quietly
safely	stoppable
wearable	workable

Powerful Protector

1. capable of being believed	
2. in a bad manner	
3. capable of being stopped	
4. capable of being broken	
5. in a quiet manner	
6. capable of being worked	
7. in an honest manner	
8. in a brave manner	
9. capable of being moved	
10. in a safe manner	
11. capable of being worn	
12. in a clear manner	

For Every Learner™: Reading & Vocabulary • ©The Mailbox® Books • TEC61187 • Key p. 80

Note to the teacher: Use with "Powerful Protector" on page 62.

63

Cleaning Up

Read each meaning.
Write the matching word in the crossword puzzle.
(Hint: Each word will end in *-able* or *-ly*.)

Across

2. in a kind manner
4. in a sweet manner
7. in a glad manner
9. capable of being loved
10. capable of being enjoyed
11. capable of being walked

Down

1. in a firm manner
3. capable of being removed
4. in a sad manner
5. capable of being treated
6. in a rude manner
8. capable of being washed

A Look at the Weather

Read each passage.
Find the matching summary and write its letter below the passage.

2. Blizzards are winter storms. They have blowing snow and wind. Wind speeds in a blizzard are at least 35 miles per hour. Snow can pile up and cause travel problems. Blizzards occur most often in parts of the United States, Canada, and Russia.

Summary _____

1. Tornadoes are very strong storms. They are sometimes called twisters. Tornadoes tend to happen in the spring and early summer. During these storms, winds can blow over 300 miles per hour. They can last for just a few minutes or can blow for about an hour. Very strong tornadoes might lift cars or mobile homes off the ground.

Summary _____

3. Hurricanes are storms that start over warm seas. When hurricanes hit land, they bring wind, rain, and even strong waves. This can lead to uprooted trees and flooding. Hurricane winds can be more than 155 miles per hour. Hurricanes tend to form during the summer and early fall.

Summary _____

Summary List

A. Blizzards are winter storms that have blowing wind and snow. They can cause travel problems.

B. Storms can happen any time of the year. They have wind, rain, or snow.

C. Hurricanes are summer or fall storms that have wind, rain, and strong waves. They can uproot trees and cause flooding.

D. Tornadoes are spring or summer storms that have very strong winds. These winds can be strong enough to move cars or mobile homes.

For Every Learner™: Reading & Vocabulary • ©The Mailbox® Books • TEC61187 • Key p. 80

The Truth About Toucans

(Pages 66 and 67)

1. Read the passage below.
2. Circle the word that shows the topic of the passage.
3. Draw a star next to each paragraph.
4. Circle two important ideas in each paragraph that tell more about the topic.
5. Use the information to plan and write a summary on your other page.

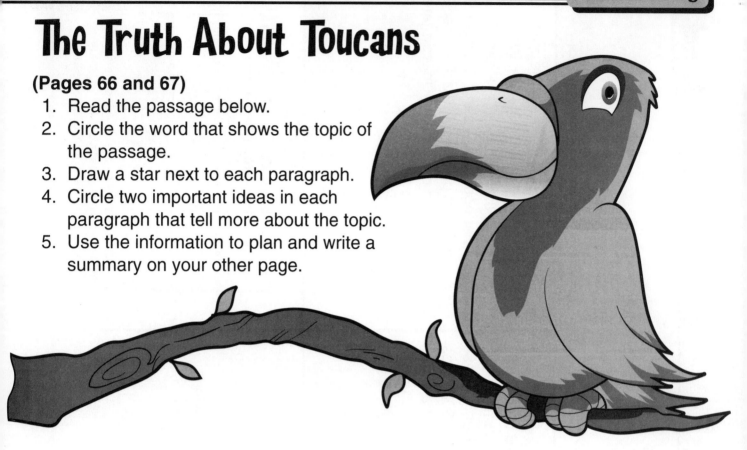

The Toucan

The toucan is a bird that lives in Central and South America. There are about 40 different kinds of toucans. Most kinds of toucans live in groups called flocks. The birds in each flock sleep in hollow trees.

A toucan has a large, colorful bill. The bill can be just about any color of the rainbow! The length of the bill helps this bird reach fruits. A toucan may also eat small animals like frogs or insects.

A female toucan has babies about once a year. She might lay one egg or as many as five eggs. The male and female toucans take turns sitting on the eggs. It takes about 15 days for the eggs to hatch. After the eggs hatch, the babies are cared for by their parents for about two months.

The Truth About Toucans

Look Back and Plan

What is the topic of the passage?

_____

List two important facts from each paragraph.
First paragraph

  1. _____

  2. _____

Second paragraph

  1. _____

  2. _____

Third paragraph

  1. _____

  2. _____

Write a Summary

Use the plan above to make your own short version of the passage. Write it on the lines below.

_____

_____

_____

_____

_____

_____

For Every Learner™: Reading & Vocabulary • ©The Mailbox® Books • TEC61187

Note to the teacher: Use with "The Truth About Toucans" on page 66.

67

Quick-Change Chameleon

1. Cut out the passage and checklist below.
2. Glue the passage to another sheet of paper.
3. Write a summary of the passage.
4. Use the checklist to check your work.
5. Glue the checklist to the back of your paper.

For Every Learner™: *Reading & Vocabulary* • ©The Mailbox® Books • TEC61187

Chameleon

A chameleon is a lizard. Most chameleons live in Africa. Some live in southern Spain and southern Asia.

A chameleon can change the color of its skin. Sometimes this happens because the chameleon is scared. Other times it is a reaction to light or temperature. A chameleon may even change colors to send messages to other chameleons. A calm chameleon may look green. An angry chameleon may look yellow.

How else can a chameleon change the way it looks? A male chameleon might puff out its throat and body if it needs to defend its feeding space. This makes it look bigger.

Writing a Summary for Nonfiction Text
Checklist

☐ I named the topic of the passage.

☐ I included important details about the topic.

☐ I used my own words.

☐ I made my summary shorter than the passage.

Peacock Pride

(Pages 69 and 70)

1. Cut apart the synonym cards below.
2. Put glue on a • on your other page.
3. Place the matching synonym card atop the •.
4. Repeat with the other cards.

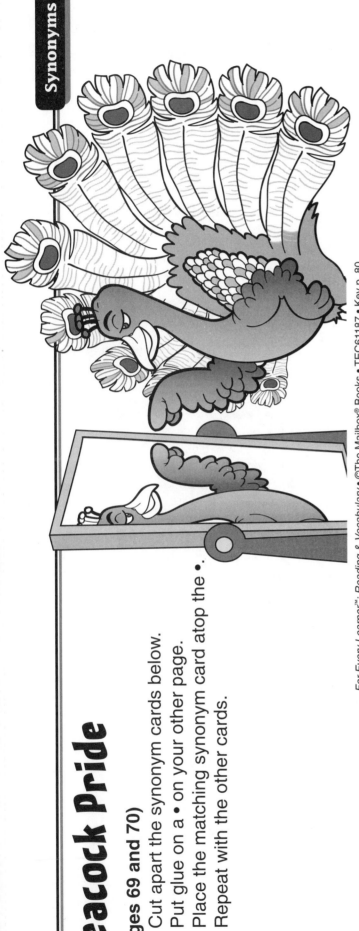

struts

displays

groomed

desire

pleased

beautiful

admire

glances

For Every Learner™: Reading & Vocabulary • ©The Mailbox® Books • TEC61187 • Key p. 80

Name

70

Peacock Pride

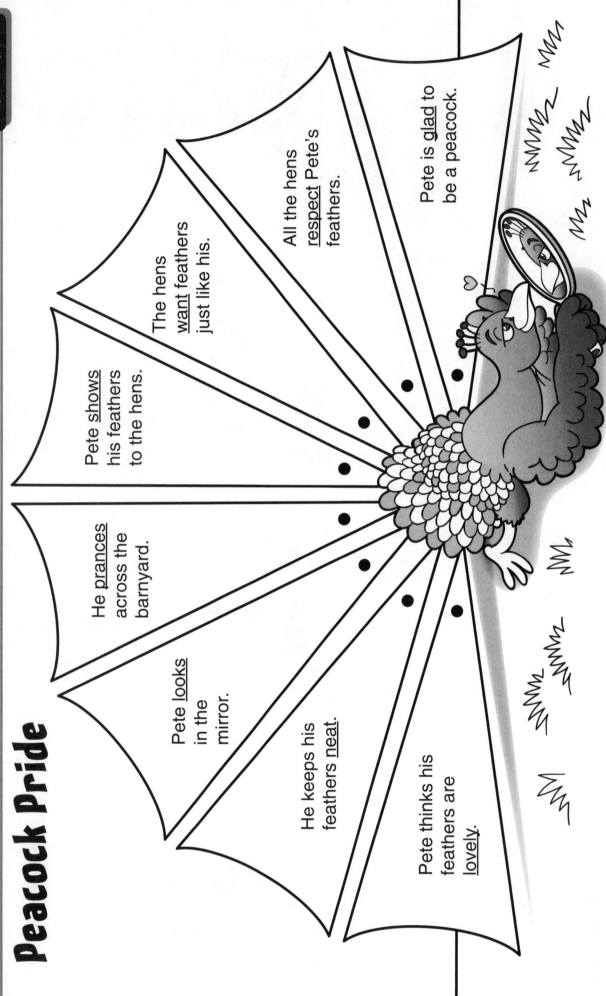

Pete shows his feathers to the hens.

The hens want feathers just like his.

All the hens respect Pete's feathers.

Pete is glad to be a peacock.

He prances across the barnyard.

Pete looks in the mirror.

He keeps his feathers neat.

Pete thinks his feathers are lovely.

For Every Learner™: *Reading & Vocabulary* • ©The Mailbox® Books • TEC61187 • Key p. 80

Note to the teacher: Use with "Peacock Pride" on page 69.

Name _____

By the Slice

Cut apart the synonym cards on the left.
Glue each card on its matching pizza slice.

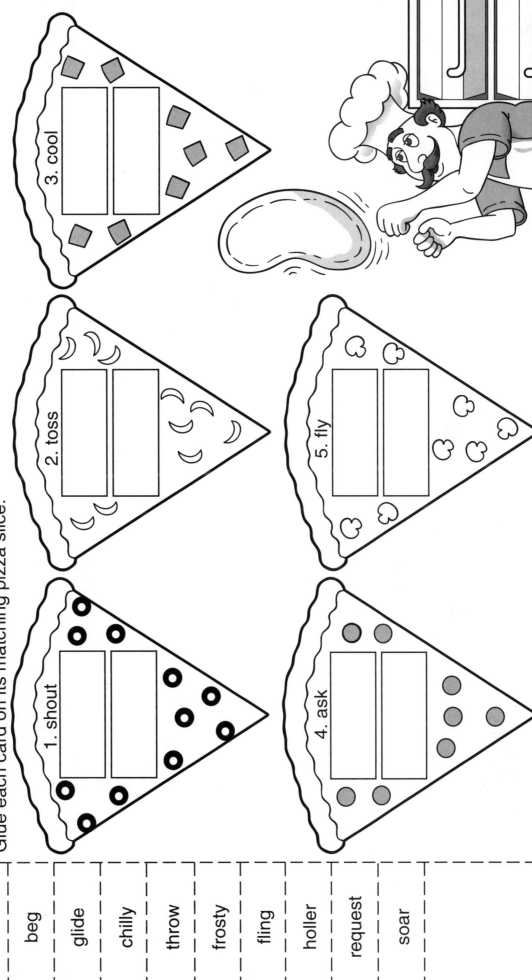

3. cool

2. toss

5. fly

1. shout

4. ask

yell

beg

glide

chilly

throw

frosty

fling

holler

request

soar

For Every Learner™: Reading & Vocabulary • ©The Mailbox® Books • TEC61187 • Key p. 80

71

Stargazing

Circle the two synonyms on each star.

1. edge center middle

2. calm quiet loud

3. divide join unite

4. keep lose hold

5. pull drag push

6. mix sort blend

7. hear sniff listen

8. near distant far

9. close shut open

10. smile grin cry

11. weak frail strong

12. dim faint bright

LUV2GAZE

Write a synonym for each uncircled word above on its matching line.
Use a thesaurus to help you.

1. _____   2. _____   3. _____   4. _____

5. _____   6. _____   7. _____   8. _____

9. _____   10. _____   11. _____   12. _____

Apple Picking

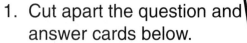

1. Cut apart the question and answer cards below.
2. Read a question and then look at the table of contents for the answer.
3. Find the matching answer card.
4. Glue the cards on another sheet of paper.
5. Repeat with the other cards.

Apples All Around Us

Table of Contents

For Every Learner™: Reading & Vocabulary • ©The Mailbox® Books • TEC61187 • Key p. 80

---

1. Which chapter might tell how an apple grows?

2. On which page does chapter 3 begin?

3. Which chapter might tell when apples began growing in the United States?

4. Which chapter might tell how to bake an apple pie?

5. On which page does "A Seed to an Apple" start?

6. What is the title of the chapter that begins on page 18?

7. On which page does chapter 1 end?

8. Which chapter might tell where apple farms are found?

chapter 1	chapter 2	chapter 4	chapter 5
page 10	page 11	page 18	"Kinds of Apples"

Surf's Up!

(Pages 74 and 75)

Directions for two players:

1. Cut apart the table of contents and key below. Then cut apart the cards on your other page and stack them facedown.
2. When it's your turn, take the top card and read aloud the question.
3. Look at the table of contents and tell in which chapter you would most likely find the answer.
4. Have your partner check your answer. If correct, keep the card. If incorrect, place the card at the bottom of the stack.
5. Continue playing until all the cards have been read. The player with more cards wins.

For Every Learner™: Reading & Vocabulary • ©The Mailbox® Books • TEC61187

Learn to Surf

Table of Contents

Answer Key

A. chapter 6
B. chapter 7
C. chapter 2
D. chapter 5
E. chapter 1
F. chapter 5
G. chapter 4
H. chapter 1
I. chapter 2
J. chapter 3
K. chapter 6
L. chapter 4
M. chapter 7
N. chapter 3
O. chapter 1

Surf's Up!

C Should surfers wear goggles?

F How does a surfer know which wave to ride?

I What can a surfer wear to avoid a rash?

L What exercises help beginners learn to stand on a surfboard?

O Is a heavy or lightweight surfboard better for beginners?

B Is Hawaii a great place for surfing?

E What kind of surfboard is best for beginners?

H What size surfboard should a young surfer buy?

K What does a surfer say when he is wiped out by a wave?

N How can a surfer stay safe while surfing?

A What does it mean when a surfer says, "Hang ten?"

D Should a surfer duck under a small wave or float over it?

G What are some exercises that help build balance?

J Is it safe to surf alone?

M Where are the biggest waves in the world?

For Every Learner™: Reading & Vocabulary • ©The Mailbox® Books • TEC61187

Note to the teacher: Use with "Surf's Up!" on page 74.

The Brave Knight

Write the letter of each question next to its matching chapter title.

How to Rescue a Princess

Chapter		Page
___	1 Who Can Be a Knight?.....	2
___	2 Feeling Brave	7
___	3 Trap a Dragon	11
___	4 Safety Gear	16
___	5 Knight School	19
___	6 A Call for Help	20
___	7 Search and Rescue........	24
___	8 Well-Known Rescues	25
___	9 A Job Well Done.............	29
___	10 Happily Ever After	31

A. What is the best way to trap a dragon?

B. How does a princess call for help?

C. What is the most famous rescue?

D. Are knights rewarded after a rescue?

E. How do knights become brave?

F. For how many years must a knight attend school?

G. Where does a princess live after she is rescued?

H. At what age can you become a knight?

I. Should knights wear helmets?

J. How does a knight find a princess?

Answer Keys

Page 5

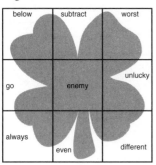

below	subtract	worst
go	enemy	unlucky
always	even	different

Page 14

1. T
2. R
3. E
4. G
5. H
6. M
7. N
8. U
9. I
10. A

THE MARINE IGUANA

Pages 6 and 7

1. north, south
2. awake, asleep
3. neat, untidy
4. huge, tiny
5. loose, tight
6. true, false
7. bought, sold
8. cheap, expensive
9. push, pull
10. east, west
11. polite, rude
12. dry, moist
13. past, present
14. male, female
15. work, play
16. spend, earn
17. multiply, divide
18. private, public
19. heavy, light
20. attack, guard
21. weak, powerful
22. possible, impossible
23. rough, smooth
24. brave, afraid

Page 8
Order may vary.

accept, refuse
agree, disagree
backward, forward
borrow, lend
careful, careless
distant, close

enter, exit
fiction, nonfiction
harmful, harmless
hero, coward
join, separate
many, few

Pages 9 and 10

1. Jake can't sleep.	He is excited about Sunday.
2. There will be a party on Sunday.	Sunday is Jake's birthday.
3. Jake's mom will bake a chocolate cake.	Jake loves chocolate cake.
4. She will put nine candles on the cake.	Jake will be nine years old.
5. Jake will blow out all the candles.	He wants his wish to come true.

Page 12

Page 13
Order may vary.

Dogs
They chew on bones and chew toys.
Their newborns are called puppies.
They pant to keep cool.
They bark, yelp, whine, and howl.

Both
They have a strong sense of smell and hearing.
They need clean water to drink every day.

Cats
They are able to climb trees.
Their newborns are called kittens.
They can walk across fences.
They purr, wail, hiss, and meow.

Pages 15 and 16
Answers will vary. Possible answers are shown.

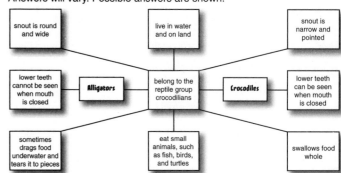

snout is round and wide

live in water and on land

snout is narrow and pointed

lower teeth cannot be seen when mouth is closed

Alligators

belong to the reptile group crocodilians

Crocodiles

lower teeth can be seen when mouth is closed

sometimes drags food underwater and tears it to pieces

eat small animals, such as fish, birds, and turtles

swallows food whole

Page 17

1. busy
2. live
3. nest
4. shed
5. protects
6. store
7. grind
8. hurry

Page 18

1. pant
2. habitats
3. hollow
4. evaporates
5. nocturnal
6. moisture
7. scorching
8. sweat

Pages 19 and 20

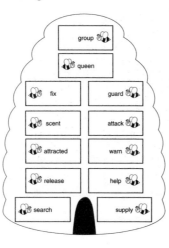

group
queen
fix
guard
scent
attack
attracted
warn
release
help
search
supply

Underlined words may vary.

1. Thousands of honeybees live and work within a **colony.**
2. Only one **female bee** in the hive lays eggs.
3. Worker bees build the hive and **repair** any cracks.
4. Worker bees also **defend** the hive's entrance from enemies.
5. A guard bee can smell the **odor** of a bee from another hive.
6. Guard bees will **swarm** a bear that may harm the hive.
7. Hungry bears are **lured** to the honey inside a beehive.
8. The guard bees **alert** the other bees of any danger.
9. Guard bees **emit** a special scent that smells like bananas.
10. The other bees **aid** the guard bees if the hive is invaded.
11. A scout bee's job is to **hunt** for food and find new hives.
12. Flowers **provide** bees with the food they need.

Pages 21 and 22

1. bee
2. shark
3. bat
4. owl
5. toad
6. snake

Page 23

1. Sea turtles use their size and fast swimming to stay safe.
2. Starfish get their name based on how they look.
3. A female lobster has a lot of eggs to increase the chances of having offspring that will become adults.
4. One way a whale is different from a fish is how it breathes.

Pages 25 and 26

Order may vary.

Facts
Fish tanks come in different shapes and sizes.
An aquarist is a person who keeps a fish tank.
Pet stores sell all sorts of fish.
There are many different kinds of fish.
Most fish should be fed at least once a day.
Guppies are one type of pet fish.
Tropical fish tanks need to be heated.
An aquarium is a container for fish.
Plants can give fish homes and food.
Fish live in either freshwater or saltwater.

Opinions
Fish tanks are easy to care for.
Colorful gravel makes a fish tank look pretty.
Goldfish are the best kind of pet fish.
Fish are fun pets to watch.

Page 27

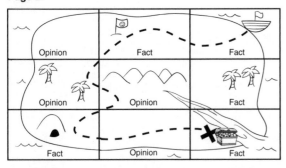

Page 28

1. green
2. green
3. yellow
4. green
5. yellow
6. green
7. yellow
8. yellow

Answers may vary.

Page 29

Order of pairs may vary.

some sum		nose knows
hear here		piece peace
so sew		right write
our hour		made maid
brake break		where wear

Page 30

T bored	A board
F wait	B weight
A where	I wear
E pair	A pear
L waste	S waist
G hair	E hare
R flour	T flower
L two	I too
N Their	H There
A knight	U night

A "BAA-LERINA"

Pages 33 and 34

Order may vary.

Life Cycle of a Butterfly
A butterfly goes through four
    stages of life.
A butterfly is an egg before it is
    a caterpillar.
A butterfly is a caterpillar before it
    forms a chrysalis.

Life Cycle of a Ladybug
A ladybug goes through four
    stages of life.
An adult ladybug lays
    eggs.
A ladybug in the larval stage
    is called a grub.

Page 35

1. rain or snow
2. rain or snow falls from them
3. in lakes
4. sun
5. Water vapor condenses
    into clouds.

Page 36

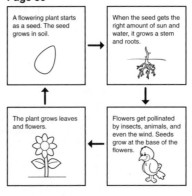

Sentences will vary. Possible answers
include the following:

Before a seed grows a stem and roots,
it needs sun and water. Before seeds
grow at the base of the flowers, the
flowers get pollinated. Before growing
flowers, a plant grows a stem and
roots. After a seed gets sun and water,
it grows a stem and roots. After a
seed grows a stem and roots, it grows
leaves and flowers. After the plant
grows leaves and flowers, the flowers
get pollinated and seeds grow.

Pages 37 and 38

Order may vary.

How Well Dogs See
Dogs cannot see all the colors
    that humans see.
Dogs are able to see moving
    objects very well.
Dogs can see well in dim
    light.
Faraway objects look blurry
    to dogs.

How Well Dogs Hear
Some dogs can hear storms that
    are many miles away.
Dogs hear high-pitched sounds
    that humans do not.
Dogs hear four times better than
    humans.
Dogs may know the sounds of
    their owners' cars.

Page 39

1. Hockey players wear helmets on their heads.
   ~~Many players have played for more than one team.~~
   Hockey players use a lot of safety gear.
   Gloves protect a player's hands.

2. ~~Goalies have to be brave.~~
   There are different ways for a goalie to stop a puck.
   A goalie can catch the puck with his glove.
   A goalie can knock the puck away with his stick.

3. A wrist shot is not as fast as a slap shot.
   The slap shot is the most powerful shot.
   ~~The puck comes at the goalie very fast.~~
   There are different types of shots in hockey.

4. Hockey is played in different countries.
   ~~The United States hockey team won a gold medal in 1980.~~
   The United States has many hockey teams.
   Canada is known for its hockey teams.

Page 40

Main idea sentences will vary.

Circus clowns ride
    unicycles.
Amazing clowns juggle balls
    and pins.
Some circus clowns walk
    on stilts.
Circus clowns all squeeze
    into a small car.

Chimps ride on bicycles
    around the ring.
Tigers jump through fire
    hoops.
Elephants walk in a line with
    their tails and trunks hooked.
Sometimes dogs jump rope
    at the circus.

Page 41

1. S
2. I
3. K
4. R
5. T
6. N
7. H
8. O

<u>HONK ITS HORN</u>

Page 42
Order may vary.

park 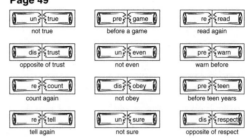	We saw a ball game at the _____. He will _____ the car in the lot.	fan	The _____ keeps us cool. Tim is a _____ of baseball.
play	Who wants to _____ baseball? The class put on a _____.	pitcher	She fills the _____ with water. The _____ threw a fastball.
swing	Kim will _____ the bat. Will you push me on the _____?	slide	The skater will _____ across the ice. Jen slid down the _____.
safe	The money is kept in a _____. The runner was _____ at first base.	coach	Our soccer _____ is the best. My dad will _____ the team.
fair	Sam won a goldfish at the _____. The team played a _____ game.	batter	Mom mixed the cake _____. The last _____ hit a home run.

Pages 43 and 44

Crossword puzzle answers:
¹foot, whip, ²pi, pa, po, ³present, ⁴bit, ⁵s, w, c, nt, ⁵match, ⁶r, n, l, ⁷l, ⁶load, ll, i, ⁷toast, g, s, w, t, h, ⁸beat, w, t, o, ⁹counter, w, r, l, y

Page 45
Order may vary.

Singular		Plural	
	<u>lion</u>'s mane		<u>cows</u>' barn
	<u>turkey</u>'s wattle		<u>goats</u>' mountain
	<u>kangaroo</u>'s pouch		<u>bats</u>' cave
	<u>crab</u>'s shell		<u>bears</u>' den
	<u>hen</u>'s egg		<u>frogs</u>' pond

Pages 46 and 47

- student's homework
- teachers' lounge
- class's pet
- teacher's bag
- bus drivers' parking lot
- principal's office
- students' teacher
- parents' meeting
- visitor's badge
- nurse's ice pack

Page 48

1. H
2. F
3. S
4. R
5. G
6. E
7. T
8. I
9. O
10. N
11. K
12. U

<u>HE FORGOT HIS TRUNK.</u>

Page 49

un true	pre game	re read
not true	before a game	read again

dis trust	un even	pre warn
opposite of trust	not even	warn before

re count	dis obey	pre teen
count again	not obey	before teen years

re tell	un sure	dis respect
tell again	not sure	opposite of respect

Page 52

dis-	pre-	re-	un-	re-pre-	dis-un-	un-re-pre-
belief	caution	paint	easy	wash	able	cut
honest	bake	trace	aware	test	like	wrap
agree	call	call	fair	plan		paid
loyal	try		happy	heat		
	copy		lucky	season		
			certain	number		

Page 55
Order may vary.

True
Jamie is three years older than Jenna.
Jenna's birthday is in the summer.
Jenna learns how to dribble the basketball.
Jenna wishes to play basketball like Jamie.
The girls play a game of basketball.
Jenna learns to play basketball at the park.

False
Jamie doesn't think she will make the team.
Jamie wants to try out for the team.
Jenna learns the wrong way to pass.
Jamie scores two more points than Jenna.
Jenna teaches Jamie to play basketball.
Jamie thinks Jenna is not a very good player.

Page 56

1. Trevor
2. Main Street
3. six days
4. He takes extra good care of the cars.
5. He lathers the car with soap.
6. warm water
7. brand-new
8. His customers are happy.

Page 57

1. Early one morning, Sue went into the garden.
2. First, she crawled over a tall fence.
3. Next, Sue slid across some rocks.
4. Then she climbed up a flower stem.
5. Later, Sue hid under a leaf.
6. Finally, she rested in the shade.

Page 58

1. As soon as Sam wakes up, he brushes his teeth.
2. First, he holds his toothbrush with one fin.
3. Next, Sam squeezes toothpaste onto his toothbrush.
4. Then he puts the toothbrush in his mouth.
5. Sam moves the toothbrush gently across his teeth.
6. Before Sam spits out the toothpaste, he brushes his gums.
7. Finally, he rinses his mouth with water.
8. Sam smiles in the mirror to see his clean teeth.

Pages 59 and 60

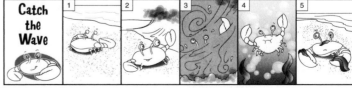

Sentences will vary.

Page 61
Order may vary.

-able	-ly
break**able**	loud**ly**
mov**able**	neat**ly**
teach**able**	quick**ly**
train**able**	slow**ly**
wash**able**	soft**ly**
wear**able**	wise**ly**

Pages 62 and 63
1. believable
2. badly
3. stoppable
4. breakable
5. quietly
6. workable
7. honestly
8. bravely
9. movable
10. safely
11. wearable
12. clearly

Page 64
Across	Down
2. kindly	1. firmly
4. sweetly	3. removable
7. gladly	4. sadly
9. lovable	5. treatable
10. enjoyable	6. rudely
11. walkable	8. washable

Page 65
1. D
2. A
3. C

Pages 69 and 70
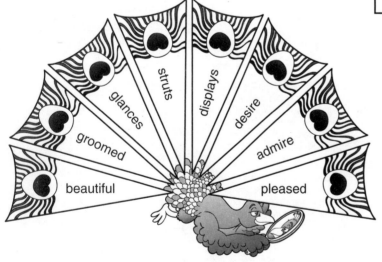

glances struts displays desire groomed admire beautiful pleased

Page 71
Order may vary.
1. yell, holler
2. throw, fling
3. chilly, frosty
4. beg, request
5. glide, soar

Page 72
1. edge, center, middle
2. calm, quiet, loud
3. divide, join, unite
4. keep, lose, hold
5. pull, drag, push
6. mix, sort, blend
7. hear, sniff, listen
8. near, distant, far
9. close, shut, open
10. smile, grin, cry
11. weak, frail, strong
12. dim, faint, bright

Page 73
1. chapter 2
2. page 18
3. chapter 1
4. chapter 5
5. page 11
6. "Kinds of Apples"
7. page 10
8. chapter 4

Page 76

How to Rescue a Princess

	Chapter		Page
H	1	Who Can Be a Knight?.....	2
E	2	Feeling Brave	7
A	3	Trap a Dragon	11
I	4	Safety Gear	16
F	5	Knight School	19
B	6	A Call for Help	20
J	7	Search and Rescue........	24
C	8	Well-Known Rescues	25
D	9	A Job Well Done............	29
G	10	Happily Ever After	31